DEC 0 3 2014

WITHDRAWN

EXPLORING THE GREAT LAKES

# HISTORY
## OF THE GREAT LAKES

Gareth Stevens
PUBLISHING

BY EMILY JANKOWSKI

**Please visit our website, www.garethstevens.com. For a free color catalog of all our high-quality books, call toll free 1-800-542-2595 or fax 1-877-542-2596.**

**Library of Congress Cataloging-in-Publication Data**

Jankowski, Emily.
History of the Great Lakes / by Emily Jankowski.
p. cm. — (Exploring the Great Lakes)
Includes index.
ISBN 978-1-4824-1205-5 (pbk.)
ISBN 978-1-4824-1191-1 (6-pack)
ISBN 978-1-4824-1434-9 (library binding)
1. Great Lakes (North America) — Juvenile literature. 2. Great Lakes Region (North America) — Juvenile literature. I. Title.
F551.J36 2014
977—d23

First Edition

Published in 2015 by
**Gareth Stevens Publishing**
111 East 14th Street, Suite 349
New York, NY 10003

Designer: Michael J. Flynn
Editor: Kristen Rajczak

Photo credits: Cover, pp. 1, 7 courtesy of the Library of Congress; p. 5 (Great Lakes) Jeff Schmaltz/NASA; p. 5 (glacier) Saraporn Bamrungchart/Shutterstock.com; pp. 6, 17 SuperStock/Getty Images; p. 9 SF photo/Shutterstock.com; p. 10 courtesy of Library and Archives Canada; p. 11 courtesy of the NOAA; pp. 13, 19 (map) Rainer Lesniewski/ Shutterstock.com; p. 15 http://en.wikipedia.org/wiki/File:Battle_erie.jpg; p. 16 Olinchuk/ Shutterstock.com; p. 19 (Niagara Falls) jgorzynik/Shutterstock.com; p. 21 Theodor Kaufman/The Bridgeman Art Library/Getty Images; p. 22 http://en.wikipedia.org/wiki/ File:Second_Baptist_Church_of_Detroit_Michigan.jpg; p. 23 Dr_Flash/Shutterstock.com; p. 24 Keystone Features/Hulton Archive/Getty Images; p. 25 Bobby Bank/WireImage/ Getty Images; p. 27 Kenneth Sponsler/Shutterstock.com; p. 29 John McCormick/ Shutterstock.com.

Printed in the United States of America

CPSIA compliance information: Batch #CS15GS: For further information contact Gareth Stevens, New York, New York at 1-800-542-2595.

# CONTENTS

Words in the glossary appear in **bold** type
the first time they are used in the text.

# WHAT ARE THE GREAT LAKES?

The Great Lakes are a collection of five lakes in east-central North America. They're the largest group of freshwater lakes on Earth, and they contain 20 percent of the world's freshwater. They connect to the Atlantic Ocean through the St. Lawrence River.

The Great Lakes began to form about 14,000 years ago, when glaciers moved across the region, scraping hollows in the land beneath them. The hollows filled with water over thousands more years to become the lakes we know today. The Great Lakes **watershed** includes parts of Michigan, Wisconsin, Minnesota, Illinois, Indiana, Ohio, Pennsylvania, and New York, as well as the Canadian **provinces** of Ontario and Québec.

# WHAT DO YOU KNOW ABOUT GLACIERS?

Glaciers are huge pieces of ice that form over many thousands of years. They move very slowly, and as they move, they alter the land beneath them. Glaciers cover about 10 percent of Earth's land and are found on almost every continent.

Lake Superior

Lake Huron

Lake Ontario

Lake Michigan

Lake Erie

The five Great Lakes are Lake Erie, Lake Ontario, Lake Michigan, Lake Superior, and Lake Huron.

# NATIVE AMERICANS

Native Americans arrived in the Great Lakes region thousands of years before any Europeans. About 120 groups of Native Americans have occupied the Great Lakes region over the course of history, including Woodland and Algonquin tribes. They used the lakes for fishing and travel as well as recreation.

Two major present-day cities—Chicago, Illinois, and Green Bay, Wisconsin—occupy spots that were important trade centers. They were connected by Native American trails. Furs, food, and jewelry were traded on routes such as these all over the Great Lakes region. Today, some of these trails have become highways.

# FEEDING THE MASSES

Native American people were **self-sustaining** and used everything they caught or farmed. Being close to the lakes was important, as tribes ate a lot of fish, such as lake trout and sturgeon. They were also excellent farmers and grew corn, squash, pumpkins, and beans. They gathered food, such as wild rice, and hunted in nearby forests.

During the 1500s and 1600s, European fur traders and Native Americans were often friendly, frequently trading for goods, furs, and skins in the Great Lakes region.

# THE IROQUOIS CONFEDERACY

The Iroquois **Confederacy** was a group of Native American nations that lived in New York State. Made up of the Mohawks, Oneidas, Onondagas, Cayugas, Senecas, and later the Tuscaroras, the confederacy formed before Europeans were exploring the region. The exact date is unknown, but it was likely more than 500 years ago! The Iroquois Confederacy mainly controlled the areas around Lake Erie and Lake Ontario.

The Iroquois Confederacy had one of the earliest **democratic** governments. Each nation had representatives on the general council and a vote in important decisions. However, the American Revolution divided the nations and destroyed Iroquois land, bringing about the confederacy's end in 1779.

# LONGHOUSES: AN INTERESTING PLACE TO LIVE

Many of the Iroquois lived in longhouses, long wooden houses built by the men of the tribes. They had no windows and were narrow and rectangular. The houses were homes for extended families, including aunts, uncles, and cousins. It was common for more than 20 families to live in each one!

Longhouses still exist today. This one was built in Ontario as part of the living museum of Crawford Lake Iroquoian Village.

# A LONG, LONG TIME AGO

The first Europeans in the Great Lakes region were the French. Jacques Cartier claimed the St. Lawrence River valley for France around 1534, including present-day Montreal, Québec. The Great Lakes themselves weren't explored until about 1614 when Samuel de Champlain found Lake Huron and Lake Ontario. He made some of the best early maps of the region.

A map from 1656 of Canada and New France shows that all five lakes were known by then. French mapmakers at this time also included the many Native American lands around the Great Lakes. Tribes in the area taught explorers such as Champlain about the land the Europeans were seeing for the first time.

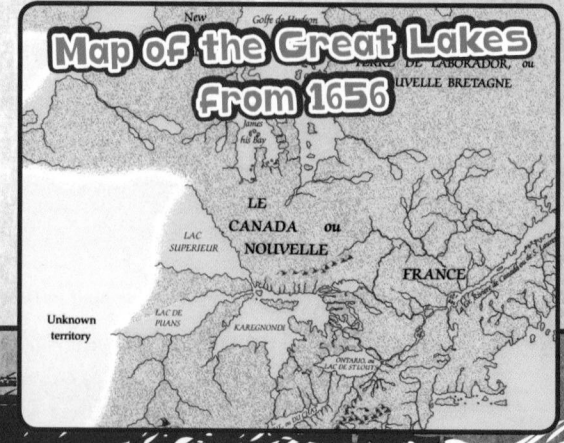

Map of the Great Lakes from 1656

# LE GRIFFON

One French ship, *Le Griffon*, disappeared while exploring the Great Lakes! Built on the shores of the Niagara River in 1679, *Le Griffon* was captained by Robert de la Salle. De la Salle sailed the ship across Lake Erie and Lake Michigan before sending it back to the Niagara River with a small crew. It was never seen again.

Shipwrecks have occurred in all five of the Great Lakes. The *Van Valkenburg*, a shipwreck in Lake Huron, is shown here being explored by a diver.

# STRUGGLE FOR THE OHIO RIVER VALLEY

The French and Indian War (1754–1763) started as a struggle for who would control the land west of the Allegheny Mountains in the Ohio River valley. The French had settlements west of this area, while the British colonies grew to the east. Both empires thought they had a claim to this land.

Many battles involving the French, British, and each country's Native American **allies** took place in the Great Lakes states of Pennsylvania, New York, and Ohio. The British eventually defeated the French, winning not only the Ohio River valley, but Canada, too. England became the ruling country of the Great Lakes region.

## THREE SIDES

The French and Indian War was part of a global conflict between France and England. Both nations wanted to increase the size of their empire by colonizing. In North America, Native American tribes fought on both sides. However, the tribes of the Great Lakes and beyond didn't want their land colonized by anyone!

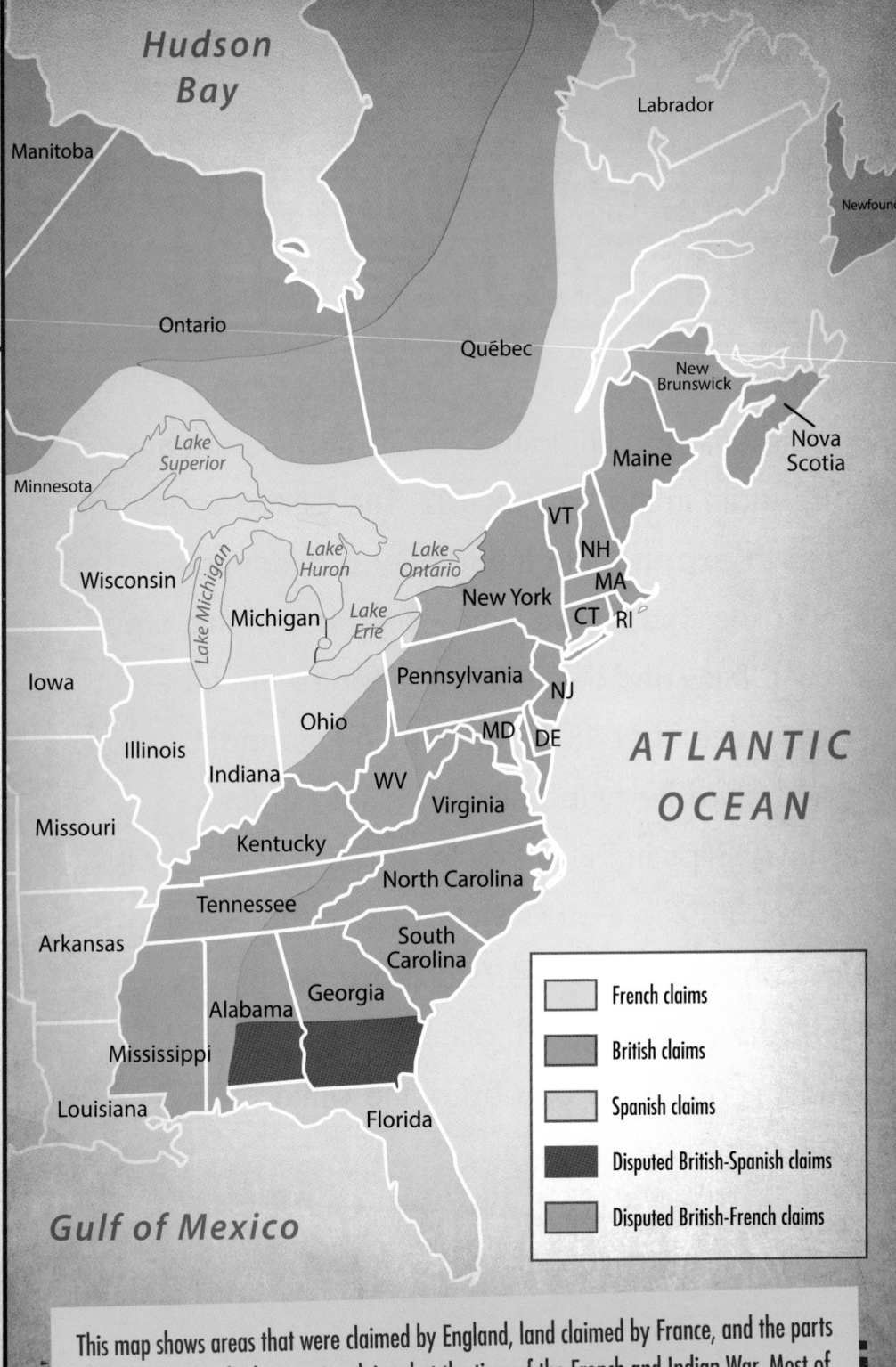

Hudson Bay

Manitoba

Labrador

Newfoundland

Ontario

Québec

New Brunswick

Nova Scotia

Maine

Minnesota

Lake Superior

VT

NH

Wisconsin

Lake Michigan

Lake Huron

Lake Ontario

MA

Michigan

Lake Erie

New York

CT

RI

Iowa

Pennsylvania

NJ

Illinois

Ohio

MD

DE

**ATLANTIC OCEAN**

Missouri

Indiana

WV

Virginia

Kentucky

Arkansas

Tennessee

North Carolina

South Carolina

Alabama

Georgia

Mississippi

Louisiana

Florida

**Gulf of Mexico**

| | French claims |
| | British claims |
| | Spanish claims |
| | Disputed British-Spanish claims |
| | Disputed British-French claims |

This map shows areas that were claimed by England, land claimed by France, and the parts of North America both countries claimed at the time of the French and Indian War. Most of the land around the Great Lakes was claimed by the French by the mid-1700s.

# THE SECOND WAR FOR INDEPENDENCE

Though the American colonies became independent from England in 1783, the two nations fought again in the War of 1812. The United States wanted to **expand** into the frontier around the Great Lakes. The Native American tribes in this area opposed this—and the British supported the tribes.

In September 1813, Master Commandant Oliver Hazard Perry led nine US ships against British warships in Put-in-Bay, a part of Lake Erie off the coast of Ohio. Perry's victory gave the United States control of Lake Erie and drove the British out of Detroit, Michigan. It also ensured that Ohio and Michigan would be part of the United States following the war.

# TREATY OF GHENT

The War of 1812 ended on December 24, 1814, with the Treaty of Ghent. It was agreed that some of the British-held land in the Great Lakes region would become part of the United States and the British would no longer have ties to Native American tribes there. Parts of present-day Canada remained under British control. The treaty resulted in the later establishment of the Canadian border, too.

The Battle of Put-in-Bay is sometimes called the Battle of Lake Erie. Master Commandant Oliver Hazard Perry is still honored around the Great Lakes today with statues in Buffalo, New York, and Cleveland, Ohio.

# THE ERIE CANAL

In order to connect the Great Lakes to the East Coast, a canal was built to transport people and goods. The Erie Canal connects Lake Erie to the Hudson River. Construction started in 1817, and the canal was completed in 1825.

Many cities in New York State grew because of their location on the Erie Canal, including Buffalo, Rochester, and Syracuse.

The building of the Erie Canal was a milestone in the history of the Great Lakes region because it allowed the movement of goods, such as farm produce, from the Great Lakes states all the way to New York City. US products no longer had to be shipped down the St. Lawrence River, which runs through Canada and was part of the British Empire.

## PRESERVING THE UNION

The Erie Canal may have influenced the outcome of the Civil War! Since the Erie Canal allowed goods to be transported from the Midwest, states such as Ohio, Illinois, Indiana, Michigan, Wisconsin, and Minnesota supported the northern states and remained part of the Union during the war. This was because so much trade was made possible between these Great Lakes states and the East Coast.

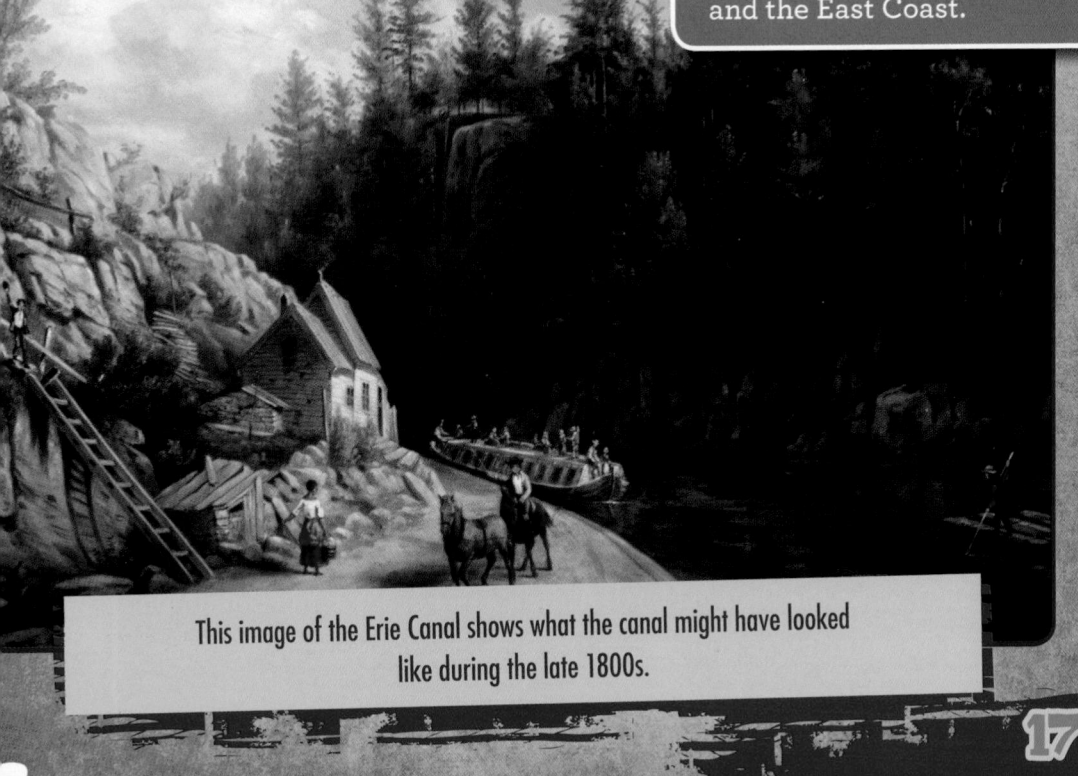

This image of the Erie Canal shows what the canal might have looked like during the late 1800s.

# THE CANADIAN BORDER

The Great Lakes are a natural border between the United States and Canada. Four of the five lakes touch Canadian land, and the St. Lawrence River connects Québec to the region. The Canadian border was officially established in 1818. However, the British continued to claim parts of present-day Oregon until 1846, when the border was extended west permanently. Today, the United States and Canada share the longest peaceful border in the world.

The Niagara River is part of the shared border with Canada. There are many historic sites along it, such as the first fort built by the British in the late 1700s, Old Fort Erie.

## CANADA DAY

By the mid-1800s, Canadians wanted some independence from Britain. On July 1, Canadians celebrate Canada Day, the day in 1867 when the British North America Act created the Dominion of Canada. It was still part of the British Empire, but had some self-governance. In 1982, Canada became an independent nation, though its cultural ties with Britain remain.

The map above shows the US-Canadian border in red. Niagara Falls, found on the Niagara River, is part of this border.

# FREEDOM IN THE GREAT LAKES

The Great Lakes region played an important role in slaves' search for freedom before the Civil War. In the mid-1800s, slaves living in the southern states wanted to escape to the northern states and Canada, where slavery was illegal.

In order to do so, the slaves needed to travel to and through the Great Lakes states and try not to get caught by slave catchers along the way. If this happened, the slaves would be returned to their former masters, and they were frequently punished quite harshly. The Great Lakes states eventually became home to many **fugitive** slaves during this time period.

# FUGITIVE SLAVE LAW

The Fugitive Slave Law of 1850 stated that anyone who helped a runaway slave would be punished. People who met an escaped slave would have to decide whether to help the slave to freedom or follow the law and report the fugitive. While many didn't support slavery, they also didn't want to break the law.

Some northern states, including New York, passed laws that gave escaped slaves rights, even under the Fugitive Slave Law of 1850.

Many routes of the **Underground Railroad** ran through the Great Lakes region! **Abolitionists** often helped slaves follow these paths to houses and buildings where they would be safe. Many people took shelter at the Second Baptist Church in Detroit, Michigan, and the Rush R. Sloane House in Sandusky, Ohio. Other known Underground Railroad "stations" can be found throughout the Great Lakes region.

Underground Railroad activity was strong in places such as Cincinnati and Ripley, Ohio. One of the most well-known points slaves had to cross to get to the North was the Ohio River. Then, slaves traveled along Lake Erie and Lake Ontario to reach Canada.

Second Baptist Church in Detroit, Michigan

# WILLIAM GOODRIDGE

William Goodridge was born into slavery, but was given his freedom at age 16. He went on to become a businessman in Pennsylvania who helped slaves escape on the Underground Railroad. He hid slaves in his home and aboard railroad cars he owned! The William Goodridge House and Museum is in York, Pennsylvania.

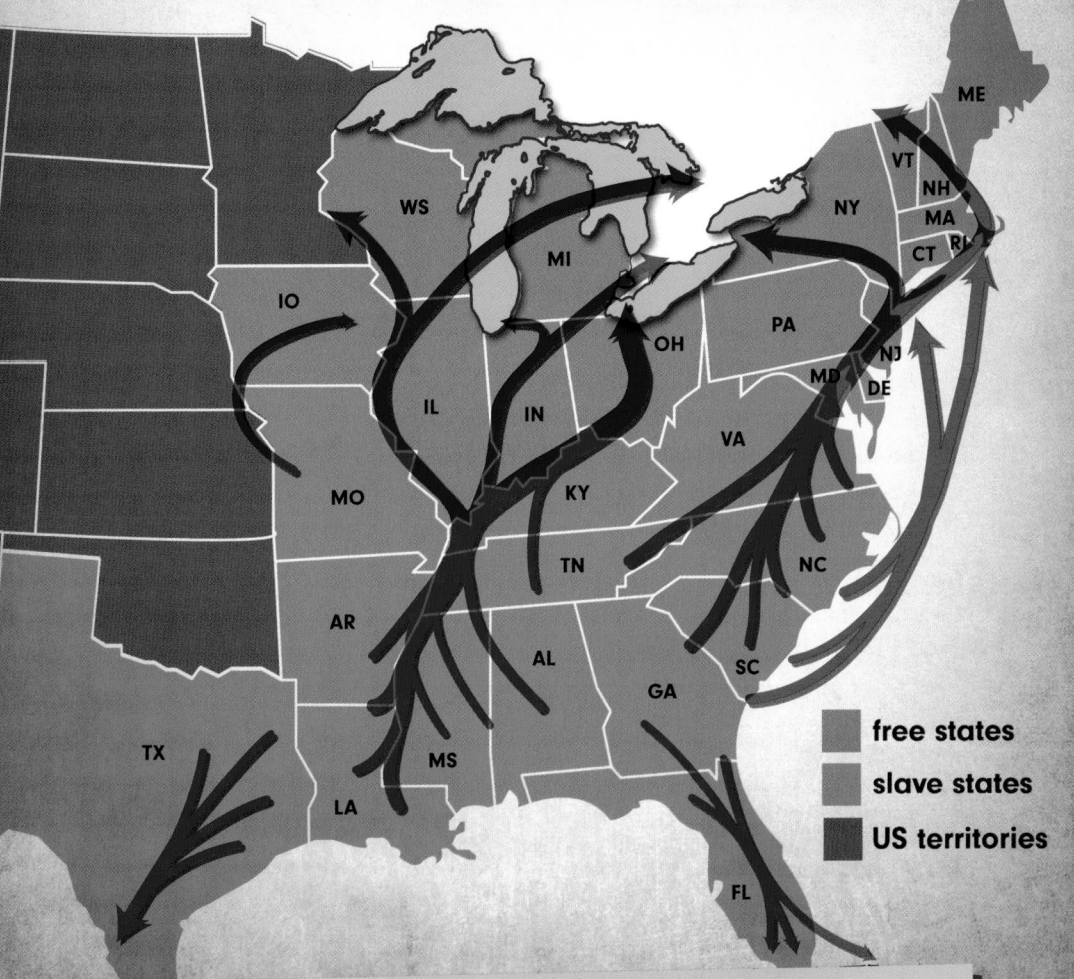

## United States in 1850

free states
slave states
US territories

This map shows many of the routes of the Underground Railroad. Slaves often traveled through the Great Lakes states to freedom.

The land around the Great Lakes has long been used for agriculture. Today, corn, soybeans, and hay are the major crops of the Great Lakes region. Commercial fishing became big business in the early 1800s, though overfishing and other problems have caused it to weaken in recent years.

Shipping in the Great Lakes began with the completion of the Erie Canal in 1825. It hasn't grown much since trucks and railroads began transporting goods in the region during the 1900s. At the beginning of the 20th century, industries such as steel boomed. Today, Detroit is still known for its automotive industry.

This image from 1903 shows the Ford Motor Company Factory in Detroit. Ford is still headquartered in the city today.

# THE RUST BELT

The term "Rust Belt" refers to the area of the Great Lakes that used to be dominated by industry. Today, many of the buildings and factories are abandoned and in disrepair. States considered part of the Rust Belt include Pennsylvania, Ohio, New York, Michigan, Illinois, and Indiana. The area is nicknamed the "Rust Belt" because the steel industry is no longer profitable—it has "rusted" over.

Steel plants like this one in Pennsylvania have been abandoned in many cities of the Rust Belt.

# SAVING THE GREAT LAKES

The Great Lakes are an important **resource**. They provide drinking water for about 40 million people in both the United States and Canada. In addition, the many **ecosystems** around the Great Lakes are home to thousands of kinds of plants and animals.

Because numerous factories operated in this region for many years, the waters of the lakes have been polluted, badly affecting water quality and wildlife. Runoff from farms, including animal waste and chemicals, has also polluted the water and damaged the ecosystems.

Just as the Native Americans did thousands of years ago, we depend on the Great Lakes, and it's important that we keep them healthy.

# A RIVER ON FIRE?

It became clear that pollution was a major issue when the Cuyahoga River caught fire in June 1969. The river flows through Cleveland, Ohio, on its way to Lake Erie. It caught fire because there was so much pollution in the water! This led to testing the water and working to improve its quality. The Great Lakes Water Quality Act was passed in 1972.

Groups from the Great Lakes states and Canada are working together to clean up the waterways in the region so we can enjoy the Great Lakes for many years to come.

# THE GREAT LAKES TIMELINE

The Great Lakes area is rich in history. Use the timeline as an overview of the historical periods covered in this book.

**14,000 years ago**  Glaciers begin to move and create the Great Lakes.

**1500s**  Native Americans living in the area begin to trade furs with Europeans.

**1534**  Jacques Cartier claims the St. Lawrence River valley for France.

**1614**  Samuel de Champlain locates Lake Huron and Lake Ontario.

**1679**  *Le Griffon* disappears while Robert de la Salle is exploring the Great Lakes.

**1754**  The French and Indian War begins.

**1763**  The French and Indian War ends.

**1779**  The Iroquois Confederacy is destroyed.

**1812**  The War of 1812 begins.

**1814**  The Treaty of Ghent ends the War of 1812 and awards land around the Great Lakes to the United States.

| 1818 | The Canadian border at the Great Lakes is established. The entire border was established later. |
|---|---|
| 1825 | The Erie Canal is finished, connecting the Great Lakes to the East Coast. |
| 1810–1850 | Many slaves use the Underground Railroad that runs through the Great Lakes region to escape from slavery. |
| 1850 | The Fugitive Slave Act of 1850 is enacted. |
| 1867 | The British North America Act creates the Dominion of Canada. |
| 1890s–1900s | Steel, automotive, and meatpacking industries boom, and many people move to the Great Lakes region to work in these industries. |
| 1960s | Industry begins to fail, creating the "Rust Belt." |
| 1972 | The Great Lakes Water Quality Act passes, resulting in cleaner lake water and groups working to protect the Great Lakes ecosystems. |
| 1982 | Canada gains independence. |

# GLOSSARY

**abolitionist:** someone who was against slavery and tried to free slaves

**ally:** one of two or more people or groups who work together

**confederacy:** a group formed for common action or purpose

**democratic:** describing a form of government in which the people choose leaders by voting

**ecosystem:** all the living things in an area

**expand:** to make something larger

**fugitive:** runaway

**province:** a political unit of a country

**resource:** something in nature that people can use

**self-sustaining:** independent, not needing help from anyone else

**Underground Railroad:** a system among abolitionists to help slaves escape to freedom in the North or Canada

**watershed:** the whole area that drains into a body of water

# FOR MORE INFORMATION

## BOOKS

Aller, Susan Bivin. *What Difference Could a Waterway Make? And Other Questions About the Erie Canal.* Minneapolis, MN: Lerner Publications, 2011.

Green, Cathy, Jefferson J. Gray, and Bobbie Malone. *Great Ships on the Great Lakes: A Maritime History.* Madison, WI: Wisconsin Historical Society Press, 2013.

Radomski, Kassandra. *Mr. Madison's War: Causes and Effects of the War of 1812.* North Mankato, MN: Capstone Press, 2014.

## WEBSITES

**The Erie Canal**
*glin.net/teach/history/native/native_3.html*
Read more about the building of the Erie Canal.

**Great Lakes**
*www.kidskonnect.com/subjectindex/28-places/geography/415-great-lakes.html*
This website goes into detail about many Great Lakes topics, such as information on each lake, threats to the region, and shipwrecks.

# INDEX